How to Create & Sell Your Book Through Self-Publishing

JAMES GIRARDI

Other books by James Girardi

How to Plan Out Your Web Design: The Plan Before the Plan

ISBN: 1534659013
ISBN-13: 978-1534659018

DEDICATION

I dedicate this book to all the supportive people in my world.
Anything is possible if you put your heart and soul into it.

CONTENTS

ACKNOWLEDGMENTS

To everyone, to following your heart and your dreams. Never stop learning, never stop growing.

1

WHAT IS KINDLE DIRECT PUBLISHING?

Setting goals is the first step in turning the invisible into the visible.
~ Tony Robbins

In its simplest form, Kindle Direct Publishing is a savior to all writers who want to see their labor of love turned into a book. It is one system of a few where authors can bypass traditional publishers, avoid rejection letters and save tons of money in trying to self-publish a book in the traditional manner. A person can have their work published digitally in a manner of hours.

Many famous authors were denied multiple times from publishers before getting picked up by a publishing house. J. K. Rowling is an example of an author getting denied multiple times before she was picked for her Harry Potter books.

That doesn't mean you have to be a great writer in order to make money publishing books. In a later chapter, we are going to discuss how you can produce books without having to be an author. Not all of us have the writing abilities to produce book after book. But having the knowledge in knowing where and how to get these books is so invaluable. For some of us, however, we want to fulfill our dreams of see our hard work in print.

Getting back to Kindle Direct Publishing (KDP)... So with KDP, Amazon has created a method for authors to self-publish their books on Amazon's platform at a fraction of the cost of traditional publishing companies. It's a simple process that just about anyone can learn quickly and if you keep reading this book, you will learn all the steps in detail of how to get an eBook published.

You should use KDP because it's one of the fastest growing, passive income industries happening today. By following these techniques and repeating the techniques with new books, you will soon be growing your passive income to great heights. Follow your dreams by writing a great novel or by being able to go after other dreams because of your writing.

Sales of Kindle Books are outpacing printed book sales on Amazon. Nearly one out of three Americans owns an eBook reader or tablet computer.

Before we go into the details of how to write and publish a book, let's go ahead and sign up for KDP. It's a free program, doesn't cost you anything to join. In fact it is also free to publish your eBook on KDP.

How to Sign Up for KDP

Log Into Your Amazon Account/Create An Account
If you already have an account with Amazon, then just go to www.KDP.Amazon.com and sign in. If you are new to Amazon, the click on "Sign Up" form the KDP homepage, enter your email address and select "I am a new customer". Enter your first and last name and a secure password. You will be required to provide additional information, including banking info so that you can get paid. Amazon will send your royalties directly to your bank account. Minimum EFT (Electronic Funds Transfer) is $10.00.

That's it, you are done signing up. "Uh?" are you asking yourself, "that's it?" Signing up for KDP is a simple and easy process.

The next steps for getting published on Kindle Direct Publishing will require having a book and book cover ready to go. This is the "meat and potatoes" of this book. We will learn how to pick a profitable niche, do keyword/keyword phrase analysis, create a proper title, write the book, and create a cover. At that point, we will be ready to continue with the publishing part of Kindle Direct Publishing.

2

RESEARCH A PROFITABLE NICHE

You just can't beat the person who never gives up
~ Babe Ruth

Finding something to write about is not that simple. If we look at the "romance" of writing a novel, then that novel came from somewhere inside you. Some experts give you a formula to writing a book and yes, I will be sharing a similar formula here.

However the problem I have with using a "formula" is that the writing should be something you are passionate about or at least have some interest in writing about. As we do the next step in finding a niche, try to make sure that the niche is something that you can find an interest in writing about.

Pick a Niche that Will Sell Well

We are going to use Amazon.com for our search tool to finding a good niche to write about. Go to Amazon.com and log into your account. On the left side of the screen, there is a dropdown, "Departments". From the dropdown, hover over to "Books and Audible". To the right of that, click on "Kindle Books". On the left side under "Popular Features", click on "Kindle Best Sellers". A new page opens and under "Kindle Store", click on "Kindle eBooks".

One more page opens and now you can see the top 100 best sellers based on their categories. Here is where you can get a sense of what is selling and in what categories.

Short List of the Above Steps:

1. Log into Amazon.com
2. Go to the drop-down menu on the left
3. Scroll down to "Departments"
4. Hover over to "Books and Audible"
5. To the right of "Books and Audible", click on "Kindle Books"
6. On the left, under "Popular Features", click on "Kindle Best Sellers"
7. A new page opens and under "Kindle Store", click on "Kindle eBooks"
8. One more page opens to the top 100 Best Sellers based on their categories.

How to Determine What is a Good Category to Start With?

For starters, I don't recommend picking a random topic. It would be a huge mistake to be in multiple niches at the same time. It is best to start with one category and plan to write a couple of books on various topics within that category, before you move on to other categories to write about.

When you research which niche to write about, you want to find books on the Best Seller list that rank at 30,000 or better. When a book is ranking this well, it means that the book is selling on average two copies a day. Another thing to look for is how long a best seller has been selling. You want to make sure these books have been out for at least a month. If it has been out for more than a month and is at the top of the list, it means that book is having staying power.

Currently the top 4 major markets or audience are:

- Health Market (meal plans, supplements, weight loss, exercise programs)
- Relationships (dating, marriage, kids, personal development)
- Money & Finance (investments, passive income programs, real estate, consulting)
- Career Market (professional services, education, career guidance)

Check the Competing Books in that Category

You want to pick a category that is trending but at the same time isn't flooded with other books by a bunch of other authors. It's a timing thing to get into a category that is popular and doesn't have too many books so you decide to write about that, but then by the time you get your book done and published, there are 10-15 other books in the same category hitting the "shelves" all at the same time.

An Example of Picking a Topic for your Book

Let's say you pick, "Health, Fitness & Dieting" for your category. It is a huge category and covers many topics like meal plans, fitness plans, mental wellness, etc. You shouldn't write a book on, "Health, Fitness & Dieting". It's just too broad of a topic to cover. Focus on one area within this category, let's say "Meal Plans". It has a flooded market of books, but if you narrow down "Meal Plans" to something more specific, say, "Meal Plans for Men", it is still a popular category but less competition in there. What we are doing is creating a "long-tail keyword" search, which will help us a little later on in the book when we start marketing the book.

When you get to this list of books on "Meal Plans for Men", click on a few of the books in new tabs in your browser. Then read and take notes on some of the good and bad reviews. The good reviews will let you know what the readers like about that book and the bad reviews will give you great ideas on how to make a new book even better.

Here are some actual not-so-good reviews for a couple of books that I found on the topic of "Meal Plans for Men":

> *"The recipes are super easy however they're not all that good, the book is nice though"*

> *"Bought this as a housewarming gift for a friend that does not cook and more of a gag gift. I thought the title was clever...but looking through the recipes, not very healthy."*

> *"The recipes are odd and unappetizing. So, if you want an easy to handle cookbook with yummy recipes, this one is not for you. You'd be better off stealing recipes off the back of cans."*

> *"It's a great concept. However, we were a little disappointed in the quality of the recipes. Not very healthy-high in sodium highly processed."*

Get the idea of what people are saying? Though the recipes were simple recipes, the end result was that the food didn't taste all that good and it wasn't exactly healthy either. If you opted to write a book in this area, you better make sure that the book is not only informational and useful but had better tasting recipes that were also healthier than in these books.

Can the Book Become a Series?

If the book becomes a "one and done", it will only get so far. Books that can become a series of books have a better chance of not just surviving but thriving in the eBook marketplace. Going off of our "Meal Plans for Men" idea, can you think of other books in this area that can be combined into a series? How about a "Meal Plans for Men, the Breakfast Edition"? Or how about, "Simple Meal Plans for the Man on the Go"? Or one more, how about, "Delicious but Healthy Dessert Ideas for Men"?

Thinking ahead like this will help with ideas for your book and ideas for later books. Imagine having the idea that you wanted to write a book, but now you have material for multiple books. As you are brainstorming ideas, you can also be organizing your thoughts and ideas into the next books.

I love using Excel spreadsheets. I have been using Excel spreadsheets for as long as I can remember. When I write books, I use an Excel spreadsheet to keep my chapters and topics organized. To someone who sees my spreadsheet for the first time, they might think, "What's going on with this mess"? But if you analyze the spreadsheet for a little while, you will see the method to my madness.

I use the first column for my chapter ideas. I use the second column for subtopics for those chapters. What I do is insert a row below my chapter name and then put a subtopic in. If I have 5 subtopics to discuss for that chapter, I will have 5 rows below it. Then I insert rows in-between the subtopics for my sentences. Sometimes they are just phrases or a note or a link to a website, whatever I need to put there. Once I get everything outlined, then I move to Word and start writing the book.

Can the Book Generate a Backend Income?

Backend income is income that is generated not from book sales but from other types of income streams, mainly affiliate marketing. Affiliate marketing is selling other people's products and making a commission off of it. The advantage to affiliate marketing is that you don't need to have inventory nor process any payments. Everything is done through an affiliate website or via your book. It's about building email lists and how to use them effectively, not just for selling other products, but you can use for promoting your future books.

There are many affiliate programs out there, but one simple program that is so easy to do is to become an Amazon Associate. It's easy and free and since you got this far, it's an easy integration for you. The link to the Amazon Associates program is: www.affiliate-program.amazon.com. Once you sign up, there are many YouTube video tutorials on web and a forum of other Amazon Associates willing to help and answer your questions.

What kind of products can we promote that would be considered "backend income" for our book? Back to our example of "Meal Plans for Men", we could sell/promote workout books, workout products, supplements, etc. These are things that we can soft sell through our book or on our website promoting our book. I used the term "soft sell" because you want the book to be informational, not a product catalog. If the reader thinks that you wrote the book just so you can sell them other products, it will be a turn off. But there is nothing wrong with recommending products that have helped you.

Checklist to Where We are Now:

- Signed up for Kindle Direct Publishing

- Find a profitable niche (that somewhat interests you) by researching categories on Amazon's Kindle Books area that are popular.

- Narrowed down the category by searching with a "long-tail" keyword.

- Checked to make sure that the search results in books in the top 30,000 Best Seller Rating

- Researched the reviews of some of the competing books and wrote down some notes as to what people are saying both good and bad.

- Determined that the book can be a series

- Determined that the book can generate a backend income.

3

CREATING YOUR MASTERPIECE

"If it wasn't hard, everyone would do it. It's the hard that makes it great" ~ Tom Hanks, A League of Their Own

At this point, we have done all of our research to determine our niche and topic for our book. Now we have to write our book. Writing a book is a little easier said than done. As Tom Hanks said in the movie, *A League of Their Own*, "If it wasn't hard, everyone would do it. It's the hard that makes it great". My personal opinion is that writing fiction books is tougher than writing non-fiction books, but who knows, fiction writers might feel the opposite way.

Outsource the Book Writing

There are options to writing the book. You can always outsource the entire book for someone else to write. In creating a passive income stream worth a lick, you will have to scale up your passive income business. If writing one book generates say $30 - $50 a month between book sales and backend income, then 10 books should generate $300 - $500 a month and 50 books should generate $1500 - $2500 a month. Sound impossible? Can you budget your time to write one book a month? If so, then that's 12 books a year.

In just a couple of years, you should have a steady stream of income.

Try to look at this from a business standpoint. How could you get 100 books into the marketplace the quickest? Write them all yourself or outsource the writing to other people? The greatest and richest entrepreneurs know how to get things done and they know that they can't do it all by themselves. They hire the smartest and best in the areas that they need in order to accomplish their goals.

Authors, like any other artist, want control of their work, their writings. I am no exception to this rule. Every word printed in this book has been written by me.

Would I outsource the writing of my book ideas? Absolutely, because it's a business and I am providing a product and service to my readers. Record producers don't write and sing music; they find the best to do it. Book publishers don't write books; they are in the business of promoting and selling books. Real estate agents don't build houses; they sell the houses that others have built.

Here are some websites where you can have others write your books for you:

Upwork.com
Elance.com (is an Upwork company)
eWriterSolutions.com
Freelancer.com
Writeraccess.com

If you want to find more ways to outsource the book writing and cover design, check out my article I wrote on how to outsource eBook writing:

www.jamesgirardi.com/how-to-outsource-ebook-writing-and-streamline-your-passive-income/.

I go more into detail on the services that they provide. You pay them and 'poof' there is your book. Ah, if was only that simple. You still have to do research before you have someone else write your book and you have to make sure they do what you want them to do.

Step 1: Research the Topic

Do research on the topic that you are going to write about, which should be started by now if you have been following the steps of this book. Gather information, book references, and blogs, on the topic you want to write about. Outline the chapters that you want in the book. Here is where using Excel is great. I have talked to other writers who say that they use index cards. One side of the card is the chapter name and the back of the card has the subtopics written on it.

Step 2: Go to a Website Specializing in eBook Writing

You don't have to use the websites listed above. I have no affiliation to any of them. Use a writer that has had experience already. The more reviews you can get, the better feeling you will get.

Use the adage, "you get what you pay for". Paying a bit of a premium may be better than going with a lesser price. Spell out the details of your book as well as the expected time frame for completing the book. Prices for outsourcing books range based on the number of pages you want written. You want the book to be between 8000-12,000 words. You may end up paying $100-$200 for the book, depending on page length and writer. Look at this as an investment towards future income.

Step 3: Stay in Contact

Stay in contact with the writer. Make sure they send you chapters here and there to assure that they are doing what they are supposed to do. Don't be afraid to ask for revisions.

Step 4: Read it, Proof it, Re-read it

When you get the finished product, make sure you read it. There are a lot of ghostwritten books on Kindle and a lot of them are crap, to put it bluntly. They are filled with spelling errors and grammatical mistakes and it hurts my brain to read them.

> **TIP:** Outsource the work but maintain the control. A lot of these freelance sites also offer article writing for blogs and such. A 500 word article may only cost $5 to write (check out Fiverr.com for more information). If you have 10 chapters on specific topics, outsource (10) 500 word articles.

Now you are getting 5000 words for about $50. Doing this will help you maintain more control over how the book is written as well as keeping costs down. By adding your own content, you can easily get the word count up between 8000 – 12,000 words.

Forget Outsourcing, You Want to Write the Book Yourself

Outsourcing the writing of a book is not the way to go if you are looking to establish yourself as a leader in an industry or connect with your readers on a deeper level. However, you can outsource the research of a topic to a freelancer and write the book yourself. With every book you write, start with answering these questions:

What is the goal of my book? What problem am I trying to solve for my reader?

I put that out there now because I want you to see the trees from the forest. We are building a plan to write a book, but let's not forget the ultimate purpose of the book, to help our readers solve a problem. Share the goal of the book to your readers in the introduction.

Back to writing our book; our goal is to have between 8000 to 12,000 words but more towards the 12,000 words. Any more than 12,000 and the reader may get bored. However, if you get beyond 12,000 words, consider breaking it down into 2 books. But how do you decide between 8000 and 12,000 words?

Go back to the books that you researched before. Looking at the books you researched before and out of the books that had BSR of 30,000 or better, how many pages did they have? Look at 5 books. How many pages and how many chapters did they have? Average out the chapters and pages and you will have a guide as to how many chapters and pages you need to have in your book.

Use your Excel spreadsheet and get your chapters set. Use the information from the other books to determine your chapters. DO NOT PLAGIARIZE. Make the book your own, not a copy of someone else's hard work. Organize your information into those chapters. Make sure the information flows from chapter to chapter. Set writing goals for yourself by telling yourself you will write 500 words a day. If you have a 8000 word book, you will have it finished in 16 days (not including proof reading, minor revisions and doing a book cover). Having a goal of a book a month is looking pretty realistic.

Create a Title for Your Book

Do you know that the people who write the headlines in newspaper have a more important job than the people who write the articles? It's because the headline of the article gets the readers to read the article. Same is true for your book. However, we do not just want a catchy title; we want to include some keywords into the title and subtitle and make the title sound appealing to your potential readers.

Each book should have a title and subtitle. The first word of the title should be a primary keyword; it will make it easier for your book to be found by people searching that keyword. As in earlier chapters, we talked about Meal Plans for Men. If "meal plans" is our keyword, then it works for the beginning of our title.

One of our previous ideas was a book for a breakfast edition, so a great title and subtitle would be, "Meal Plans for Men: The Breakfast Edition". Or another subtitle could be, "50 Quick and Easy Breakfast Ideas".

Let the title be a solution for your reader. More words in the title will help, but obviously do not go overboard with the amount of words. So to expand one more time on our example, we could a title like, "Healthy Meal Plans for Men: 50 Ideas for Quick and Easy Breakfast Meals for the Man on the Go".

Not only will the book rank well, but you are offering a solution to people who are looking for fast and easy, yet healthy meal plans for men.

Sample Layout for a Professionally Looking Book

The following list of pages and descriptions are your guide to make sure you include everything you need in your book. The below guide is geared more towards digital books than print on demand books.

Title Page – When you do your book cover and upload it to KDP, it will become the first page of your book. The next page will be your title page. This is where you will add your Title, Subtitle and Author's Name (you that is). It should be centered on the page. Insert a page break and begin your Copyright Page.

Copyright Page – You want to protect your work and as well not be held liable for any information in the book that causes harm. For example: If you write a work out book and someone pulls a muscle, you don't want them trying to sue you for it.

Shortcut tip: For the "©" symbol to appear, hold down the [ALT] key and then press 0169, that will make the copyright symbol appear.

Dedication Page (optional) – If you are dedicating the book to someone, here is where you would add that information.

Preface/Prologue Page (optional) – Follows the Dedication Page.

Free Bonus Page (optional) - offer something free, can be from your blog, promote your website, etc.)

Table of Contents Page (TOC) - Each chapter should be formatted as a "Heading". In the next chapter under Formatting Chapter Titles, we will go over the steps on how to format your book the right way. If you use the formatting steps for your chapters, you can have Word process your table of contents automatically.

Located under the "References" tab in Word, on the far left, there is the "Table of Contents" function. Click on it and it will start the process. Make sure the dialogue box for page numbers is unchecked. We leave the page numbers uncheck because your book will be digital on various devices so the page numbers may not match up correctly. Select "Show levels" and click "OK" and your table of contents should appear.

Set the Bookmark for your Table of Contents – Kindle allows you to set up "Go To" places in your book. It recognizes the table of contents with the "TOC" shortcut. To set it up, highlight the words "Table of Contents" in your book, then click on the "Insert" tab and select "Bookmark". In the box, type "toc" (no quotes) and then click "add".

If you start your Table of Contents before your book is done, that is OK. As long as your chapters are identified as "Heading 1", all you have to do is click anyway in your Table of Contents, then hit the F9 key and all your new chapters will be added and if there are any deleted chapters, they will be removed.

Introduction Page – Thank them for downloading your book, tell them the goal of your book and tell them a little about yourself.

Chapters 1 – X (however many chapters are in your book)

Summary/Conclusion Page – Highlight the best parts of the book and ask for an Amazon review.

More Books by Me Page (or look for my future books on "x" topic)

Glossary – If applicable

One advantage to using my Excel spreadsheet idea is that your introduction page will be similar from book to book so you can copy and paste that information from one book's spreadsheet to the next.

Let's focus on your chapters next. Let's assume you decided on 8 chapters. On your spreadsheet (or paper works too) you want to type out (write out):

Chapter Titles: Create titles to your chapters

Add subtopics: Below the respective chapters, include pertinent topics to that chapter.

Add pertinent information: Once you are happy with the flow of the chapters and subtopics, you can begin adding the pertinent information to each subtopic.

Eliminate any fluff: Get rid of information that isn't really important and may just be fluff so your word count can be higher.

Add resources: Adding resources to specific chapters is an awesome way to add value. Add related websites or any free informational content. When adding websites, you can use the "link" function within Word but if you are planning on having your book in print too, then you will have to type out the full version of the URL and remove the hyperlinks.

Planning ahead: Think about each chapter as a potential blog post for a later date. In you blog post, you aren't going to write the entire chapter, but make it enticing for your blog readers to find and buy your book.

4

TOOLS AND TIPS TO WRITING YOUR BOOK

*"Desire is the key to motivation, but it's determination and commitment
to an unrelenting pursuit of your goal – a commitment to excellence –
that will enable you to attain the success you seek"*
~ *Mario Andretti*

Writing Tools

Excel & Evernote
I like to use Excel (if you haven't already read that in this book).
Another reason for using Excel for my outline and Word for my
writing is that I save the documents to evernote.com. Google
Drive does the same thing but I started a long time ago with
Evernote so I am use to it. Evernote allows you to upload
documents, web pages, and so much more. There is even an
extension for your browser so you can save any web page to
Evernote.

You can then view or download the documents on any device that
has Evernote attached, like smartphones, tablets, laptops and
computers. I do most of my writing at home but do have the
ability to do some writing at my business. Another plus is if I'm

out somewhere and get an inspiration, I can just open up my "note" in Evernote and type it in there. Evernote is free, though they do have a premium plan too. www.evernote.com (I am not affiliated with Evernote, just sharing a valuable resource tool).

Dry-Erase Board

Another idea for doing your outline is a large dry-erase board. Write the goal of the book in the middle of the board and circle it. Draw lines from the circle heading away and then write the chapters at the end of the lines. Circle the chapters and then draw lines away from the circles with the sub-topics. Then you can write notes and such. May look a little messy but if it works for you, then by all means use it.

Scrivener

A lot of authors love this software. It takes my Excel spreadsheet to all new levels. It's not a free software and I have not personally used it but many authors have and swear by it. www.literatureandlatte.com/scrivener.php

Calibre

Calibre is a free, open source eBook library management application. You can convert your eBooks to various types of formats, sync to eBook readers, eBook editor and more. It is free to use and you can visit their website at: www.calibre-ebook.com.

Formatting Tips for Using Word

There is one important tip I can give about formatting your book in Word. Do not click the 'enter' key twice to make space between paragraphs. Clicking 'enter' twice might look ok in Word, but in some other programs, the programs recognize the 'enter' key as a new paragraph so if you click 'enter' twice, it will look like there is an empty paragraph.

Instead follow these directions:

Formatting Chapter Titles
1. Type out your Chapter Title
2. Highlight the Chapter Title

3. Right click on Chapter Title while it is still highlighted

4. Scroll down to "Styles"

5. Move to the right to open the window

6. Scroll down to "Update Heading 1 to Match Selection"

7. Next go back to "Home"

8. Scroll to the right to "Change Styles" and click on the down arrow

9. Go to "Heading 1" and click on the down arrow and go to "Modify"

10. You can modify the spacing between the Chapter Title and the first paragraph of the chapter.

Formatting Paragraph Spacing

1. From the top of Word, scroll over to "Page Layout"

2. In the middle of the top, you will see "Paragraph" with an arrow pointing to the lower right. Click on that.

3. In this screen, you can modify the spacing between paragraphs so you don't have to click "enter" twice when you want to add an empty space between paragraphs. I usually set it to 12 pts after the end of the paragraph.

Other Formatting Tips

1. Avoid using a tab at the beginning of a new paragraph

2. Use a page-break at the end of each chapter so the new chapter will start on a new page

3. Do not copy & paste images into your book, instead use the "Insert" feature within Word

4. Do not use page numbers in the Table of Contents or on the pages of the book since the pages will be in different sizes based on different readers.

5. Use generic font (like Arial or Times New Roman) and font sizes (10-12 pts).

6. Leave margins alone as well.

Tips to Get your Book Done in a Timely Manner

Set a Deadline for Yourself

One book a month; it's a realistic deadline and one that you can follow easily on a calendar. If you finish early, you can take some time off or start researching the next book. It is whatever works for you. Use an Excel spreadsheet, use Google Calendars, use whatever keeps you focused on the prize.

Set a Master deadline for the book, but also set mini-deadlines for doing the research, the outline, the chapters, content, book cover, publishing and last promoting. For visual people, it helps a lot to see it laid out like that.

Be consistent

We all have work commitments, family commitments, hobbies and other things that get in the way with getting your book done. For me, I have web design clients that I do during the day and then another business that I run at night. I have found that early Saturday and/or Sunday mornings work best for me to knock out some writing. It's quiet around the house and even more beneficial; it seems that my mind is quiet at those times too.

When I do sit and write, I can do between 1000-1500 words at a time. So I am still on target to do a book a month. I do have the opportunity during the week to do research on topics and content and such but it's hard for me to get that "quiet" time I so desperately need.

Keep your eye on the goal of the book

Keep asking yourself, why you are writing the book? If you say just so you can make money, well then close this book and find one entitled, "How to Make Millions in a Month". Let me know how you make out with that. However if you stay focused on the goals of the book, it will keep the creative juices flowing.

First drafts, second drafts, it doesn't matter

Get your first draft done. I have fallen into the trap of writing a chapter or two, but then the next time I sat down to write, I redid the beginning chapters and only did a little new work. Over time my first chapters, in my opinion, felt like they were better written than my later chapters (this book is not included in this trap). Get your first draft done then go back and start reviewing and revising your chapters.

Read and Re-read, Run Spell Check

There is nothing worse than reading an eBook that has grammatical and spelling errors in it. It makes the book look cheap and it makes the industry look cheap. Make sure you run spell check and have another person or two read the book and be specific in asking them to check for any type of errors in the book.

Care about what you are writing about
If you care about what you are writing about, then your readers have a better chance of caring about your book. Remember the title of this chapter, "Creating Your Masterpiece". You can't create something magnificent if you don't care to create it. Put your blood, sweat and tears into your creations, you won't be sorry you did.

So many people wish they could write a book. You are actually going to do it. You are in an elite group of people who can actually say that. I remember back when I wrote my first book, I was told that it wasn't real because it was an eBook. After I chuckled inside, I did feel offended but at the same time felt that the person was probably a bit on the jealous side. As they say, "haters are going to hate".

I can recall a story many years before my first book; it was when I opened my first business. We were barely making any money, but I knew that if we got a good break, we would soon be on our way. At a family gathering, people asked, "How's business"? I said, "Good, things are moving in the right direction". After some more follow up questions and answers, I had mentioned that it was my goal to get my pilot's license and one day fly between our offices (I ended up having 4 offices in 3 different states). When I mentioned my goal of getting a plane and flying between the offices, my aunt laughed and said, "Yeah right, you are going to get a plane and fly around to your offices"?

I told myself, "No I'm going to get a helicopter and land it right on your house". Within the first 2 years of opening the business, I ended up getting my pilot's license, a plane and I used to fly it between my 4 offices. The point of this is not to brag to you about how I had a plane and used it to fly around but to let you know that anything is possible if you create goals, create deadlines and truly care about what you are doing.

5

YOUR BOOK IS DONE, WHAT'S NEXT?

Know what you want to do, hold the thought firmly, and do every day what should be done, and every sunset will see you that much nearer to your goal.
~ Elbert Hubbard

Now that you have your book written, we still have some work ahead to get the book from computer to the public.

Output your Book into HTML

It's not as hard as it sounds, especially if you are using Word to write your book. In Word, do the following:

Go to >> File >> Save As >> Web Page, Filtered

If Word prompts with a warning about "remove office tags", click "Yes". If your book has images, then you will need to create a compressed file. In the folder that your book is saved as a Filtered Web Page, there should be another folder with the images. Right click on the HTML file and scroll to "Send to" and then go to

"Compressed (zipped) folder". A new folder will be created. Drag and drop your images folder in there as well.

After we complete some more steps, we will upload the book to Amazon, but for now, this is how you would output the book.

Create Your Cover

Whoever said, "Don't judge a book by its cover", didn't apply to eBook publishing. Covers are so important to getting people to look at your books. The picture IS worth a thousand words, but even more important, it could be worth a thousand dollars to you. Like outsourcing book content, you can outsource the book covers. In fact, many authors will agree that if you don't know how to use any graphic software packages, then definitely plan to outsource your book covers.

On the KDP site at Amazon, you can create a book cover using their book cover creator. It's not the most creative tool in the world but gets the job done and it doesn't cost a thing to use.

However, if you are familiar with Photoshop or Illustrator or InDesign, the by all means create it on your own. Here are some guidelines to follow:

- Research other book covers in the same niche to gather ideas on what works and what doesn't

- Book cover sizes should be 3000px x 4500px

- Use high resolution pictures, if applicable to your design

Here are some color schemes and how they relate to viewers:

> Red – Energy, enthusiasm, emotion, power
> Orange – Positive, dynamic, confident
> Yellow – Ambition, motivation
> Green – Nature, vitality, environment, health
> Blue – Dependability, trust, calmness
> Dark Purple – Depth, mystery, fantasy
> Grey – Sophistication, knowledge, wisdom

Pink – Youth, playfulness, emotion
Black – Authority, power, mystery, suspense
Brown – Natural, earthy, comfortable, organic

Even though you are creating a large cover in say Photoshop, people are going to be viewing it on Amazon and it will be smaller than what you created so definitely test it out by viewing the cover as a small image to see how it looks.

Outsource Your Cover

You have opted not to design your own cover and want to outsource it. One great resource to go to is, www.selfpubbookcovers.com/index.php. For only $69, you browse 100's of covers and pick one that is just right for your book. And beauty of it is that once a cover is used, it can't be used by another author. You fill in the information of your book online and get your cover. *I am not affiliated with this website.*

There are other resources for your book covers too:

www.fiverr.com
www.guru.com
www.elance.com
www.99designs.com/book-cover-design

If you are having trouble deciding between doing the cover yourself or outsourcing, then outsource the cover. Remember that the title on your title page in your book must match the title on your book cover.

Deciding on a Pen Name

There are two thought processes on using pen names for your books. Some people set up separate pen names and use for different categories. You can have up to 5 different pen names in your Amazon account. The reason for this is that you are trying to become an authority in a particular field and it may not look like you are an expert in one field if you have books in multiple fields.

Other people follow a different theory and use one pen name for all their books. Their reason behind this is that if people like you as an author and trust your knowledge in one field, you may be able to cross-sell them into your other books. The thought behind it is let's say you have 3 or 4 books in one field and then you decide to focus on another field with a different pen name, then your new pen name would have to start all over again becoming an authority figure in a new field.

What I have done is use one pen name for a couple of categories in the non-fiction arena, but use a different pen name for the fiction books that I'm writing. Whichever way you choose, there really isn't a right or wrong way of doing it. It is more of a preference that you are comfortable in doing.

6

PUBLISHING YOUR MASTERPIECE

My goal was never to just create a company. A lot of people misinterpret that, as if I don't care about revenue or profit or any of those things. But what not being just a company means to me is not being just that - building something that actually makes a really big change in the world.
~ Mark Zuckerberg

Here comes the magic time; not too corny I hope. Back in Chapter 1, we created an account at Kindle Direct Publishing. Now it's time to put that to use so that we can publish the book.

13 Steps to Publishing your Masterpiece

1. Log into your account at www.KDP.amazon.com

2. Click on "Create new title"

3. Enroll this book in KDP Select?
It's an important option so please read carefully

PROs:

KDP Select is a program where your book has the potential to reach more readers. However with each 90-day enrollment period, your book is exclusive to Kindle which means you cannot sell it anywhere else, including your own website.

In KDP Select, you book is available to the Kindle Unlimited program which allows its members to read books in the program for free (they pay a $9.99/monthly fee for the service). You get paid based on the pages they read. There is a fee schedule on the KDP website. The commissions are very low for this program. Which leads to the...

CONs:

Your book can not be sold on any other site, including your own site. You can have a link on your site back to Amazon however you cannot sell it as a .pdf or sell your book on other sites like Barnes & Noble, Apple, Smashwords, etc. And again, the commissions in Kindle Unlimited are very low. Some authors feel that their lion's share of book sales come from Amazon so they don't mind enrolling in KDP Select. I believe it is better not to put all your eggs into one basket so though I have enrolled in KDP Select, I won't be in the future.

4. Enter Your Book Details

a. Book Name: Enter your Title: Review Chapter 3 again for tips on how to create a title that sells.

b. Subtitle: Enter your subtitle: Review Chapter 3 again for tips on how to create a subtitle using keyword phrases.

c. Check or don't check, "This book is a part of a series": If yes, enter the numeric value of the book in the series.

d. Edition number (optional): If you are updating an already published book, then enter the new edition number.

e. Publisher (optional): KDP is not the publisher, so if you are working on your own, enter your name here.

f. Description using HTML: Very important section. Here is where you are selling your book to people viewing it on Amazon. You can use basic HTML to format the section. I have a list of HTML Tags that you can use and how to use them on my blog. Use a headline for the book. Enter the reasons to make your book an essential part of your book topic. Do some bullet points as a preview of the topics that will be covered. Finish it with a call-to-action, asking your potential readers to download your copy today to start learning [enter your topic].

Research some of the competing books and see how they write and what they write in their descriptions.

g. Add Contributors: add anyone else that helped you with the book, like a co-author or an illustrator.

h. ISBN (optional): An International Standard Book Number (ISBN) is like a serial number for a book. It helps bookstores and libraries identify your book. It's used by all the major search engines. A single ISBN costs $125.00, however if you plan to write multiple books, you can purchase ISBNs at a deep discount. However to publish on Amazon, it's not necessary to purchase an ISBN. Amazon assigns a number using their system called, ASIN.

If you are planning on trying to sell your book directly to book stores, then you will definitely need an ISBN.

5. Verify Your Publishing Rights
You are verifying that you have the right to publish this book and that it's not a public domain work.

6. Target Your Book to Customers
a. Categories: Pick the category that best matches the topic of your book. But also pick another category that may be only slightly related as well. If your main category is a very wide category, it may be hard to get ranked high, however if you use another category as well, that isn't as big, you have a bigger chance of moving up the ranks quicker in a slightly related category.

b. Age Range: Use the age range only if you are publishing a book geared towards children.

c. U.S. Grade Range (optional): Also geared towards grade levels. If you are publishing a book for children, there is more information about the guidelines for publishing children's books on the KDP website.

d. Search Keywords/Keyword Phrases (up to 7): Here is where you can add more keywords and phrases to boost your book's ability to be found on Amazon. Amazon suggests not using a keyword that you already used for a category choice. For example, if we use our Meal Plans for Men idea, a category we would want to be in would be, "Health, Fitness & Dieting" and "Nutrition". Keywords and phrases that we would use would not include those 4 words. You have the ability to add up to 7 phrases and you need to spend some time thinking and planning about the Categories and the Keywords/Phrases.

7. Select Your Book Release Option (ready to sell vs. pre-order)

The main advantage to doing a "pre-order" is that you can promote your book up to 90 days in advance. All pre-order sales count towards your sales rank. However your book won't be released to the buyer until the pre-order time is over. The steps to doing a pre-order are:

a. Click the "Make my book available for pre-order"

b. Pick a release date from 5 to 90 days ahead.

c. Upload your book, book cover, book description and pricing

d. Select if your manuscript is the final version or a draft. If it's a draft, you must have the **final draft ready 10 days before the release date**. Failure to do so and you will forfeit your pre-order sales and you will not be able to do the pre-order program for one year.

e. Check everything over and start promoting your book.

If your book generates some nice pre-order sales, your book can come out with a strong sales record. Highly successful pre-orders can it the "Hot New Releases" list, giving your book even more exposure. Final tip on pre-orders, make sure you book draft is done before picking a release date.

8. Upload or Create a Book Cover: Review section 2a and 2b of Chapter 5.

9. Upload Your Book File: If your book does not have any images, then you will upload the HTML file we created earlier. If there are images, then you upload the zipped folder that you created in Section 1 of Chapter 5.

a. Enable Digital Rights Management vs. Do Not Enable Digital Rights Management: Another split debate among indies, deciding on whether or not to do DRM or not will come down to your choice. What DRM does is protect unauthorized distribution of a kindle book.

Meaning John Smith purchases your book on his Kindle and then lends the file of your book to his friend for a short period of time. Some authors don't mind, thinking that they are getting more exposure.

However, DRM also stops John from reading your book on his phone if he originally purchased it on his tablet. My recommendation is to not do DRM. Once you decide on the DRM, you cannot change it at a later date.

b. Click on "Browse" and upload your book content file.

10. Price Your Book
How much is your book worth to you? However the question really is, how much is the book worth to your readers? If you wrote a 3000 word book, it would probably fetch $0.99 in the eBook market. However if you wrote 20,000 words and it has quality content serving a purpose to your readers, then you can price it higher. Pricing is going to be based on the book, you as an author and the niche that the book is in.

These word counts are based on a non-fiction book. Fiction books can have word counts well over 100,000 and therefore warrant higher prices. But if you are an unknown author with no fan base, then you must take that into consideration. Research the price points your competitors have their books priced at and use that for a basis.

35% vs. 70% Royalties in the Kindle Store
Books priced at less than $2.99 will only qualify for 35% royalty rate. As well, books that are in the 35% royalty rate for digital books are available in all territories whereas books in the 70% Royalty Option are only available in certain territories.

11. Kindle MatchBook
This program gives customers the ability to purchase your kindle version of a specific title if they had already purchased the print version of the book. The promotional list price for the Kindle MatchBook is either $2.99, $1.99, $0.99 or free.

12. Kindle Book Lending
This program allows customers who had purchase your kindle version to lend the book to another person for a 14 day period.

13. Click on "By Clicking Save and Publish Below..."
You confirm that you have the rights to make the content available for marketing, distribution and sale.

Before it "hits the shelves", you will have the ability to preview the book to see how it looks first. Viewing on your computer, the preview screen will look like a Kindle device. Here's a great place to double check to make sure your formatting is done correctly. If everything looks good, then click the "Save and Publish" button and in a few moments your masterpiece will be available for the world to see.

What to do if your Book didn't Publish Correctly

If for some reason you do publish the book and then find errors, you can go back to the "Add Book Details" page, then click on the "Action" button and select "Edit book details". Scroll down to the section where you upload the file again and upload the latest version. Make sure you continue and click "Save and Publish" again. First time I tried to upload again, I thought the new version was live and it wasn't. It was frustrating trying to figure out why the newer version wasn't going live.

If customers have already purchased your book before the modifications were done, you can contact Amazon and alert them of the situation. Make sure you give Amazon details to titles, examples of corrections, etc. After a review process, Amazon will send an email to the people who have previously purchased the book and let them know that they can do an update of the book through their Kindle page.

Congratulations! You have published a book. But your job isn't done yet.

7

LAUNCHING YOUR BOOK

Things do not happen. Things are made to happen.
~ John F. Kennedy

The most important time for your book is the first two weeks of the book launch. If you do it right, your book will be on Amazon's bestseller list and that means Amazon will be doing some of the marketing for you. Formula for a successful book:

Paid Sales + Reviews + Free Downloads + Length of Time Period = High Best Seller Rank

3 Steps to Launch your Book

Step 1.
Launch the book at $0.99 or at whatever price you feel works best for your book. If this is your first book or if your book has less than 8000 words, then $0.99 is a good price.

Step 2.
Make it a goal to get at least 5 reviews. People like to buy things that other people have already bought. It is the mass mentality.

6 Ways to Getting Reviews for your Book

1. The fastest way to get reviews is by swapping reviews with other authors. However do not fall into "buying" reviews. There are groups that will write reviews just for the sake of writing reviews as long as you write reviews for them as well. This hurts the industry and cheapens your book.

2. You can ask family and friends to review your book but hopefully your book is something that they would find interesting, otherwise the review may seem flat or not pertinent to the topic of your book.

3. Ask eBook bloggers to write a review of your eBook. If they do, save their names and websites and hopefully they wouldn't mind sharing a link to your book on their blog.

4. Join Facebook Kindle eBook groups and ask for review swaps: Just make sure that you tell the people you swap with to wait a couple of days before writing the reviews; you don't want the review to get flagged.

5. Post your book launch on your Facebook account and add a link to your book on Amazon. We will discuss doing a pre-order strategy later on in the book.

6. Invest in a Facebook ad (optional, especially for first time books)

Step 3.
Schedule a free promotion through KDP.

6 Resources to Run Your Free Promotion

1. If you are enrolled in Kindle Select, you can run a free 5 day book promotion once every 90 days. The goal to doing this is to

try and get 10 more reviews. Best days to do the promotion are Sundays through Thursdays.

2. Either go to Fiverr.com and hire someone for $5.00 to do your promotion or you can go to various websites to inform them of your promotions. Some sites require 7 day notice for promotions on their sites so take this into account before you start your 5 day free promotion.

I have created a free guide that you can download from my website entitled, *The Ultimate Guide to Promoting Your eBook.* In the guide, there are over 100 resources to try for promoting your book from social media strategies to online book review sites. It will help with the following steps: You can get to the guide from here as well: www.jamesgirardi.com/ultimate-guide-ebook-publishing-free-guide/

3. Research and join Facebook groups and advertise on their pages.

4. Market your book on Twitter. Try not to make the tweet sound 100% like a sales pitch. I know it's only 140 characters so make them count. Here is an example of what to tweet:

"Free How-to [insert topic of book here] on Kindle. [insert link to book] #freekindle #freeebook #[insert keyword of your book]"

5. Market on Instagram, if you have an account.

6. If you are familiar with Photoshop, make an ad with your book in the middle of the ad. Here's a sample that I made for one of my books. Visit www.jamesgirardi.com/book-on-web-design/ and scroll down the page to see the ad copy.

8

WHAT COMES NEXT?

A good plan violently executed now is better than a perfect plan executed next week.
~ George S. Patton

Scale up your business by creating a few different avenues for more books sales as well as other products. By scaling up, you want to create a brand for yourself so following the next few steps are crucial towards building your brand.

7 Ways to Scale Up your Book

1. Create a Website or Blog for Your Book
When I began creating websites, I was against using WordPress, thinking it was more for bloggers than for business. However in recent years, the WordPress platform has grown by leaps and bounds and it's not just for bloggers anymore. Businesses, both big and small are using WordPress for their websites. e-Commerce businesses are using WordPress too and there are many plug-ins available to create a robust ecommerce website. I have recently moved my website from HTML to WordPress. I have written a

few articles on how to get started with WordPress, which are all on my blog.

I can't stress enough the importance of having a clean looking website. I was on a blogger's website recently and he had listed about 40 other blogger sites, with links to their respective websites. I went on to each and every one of those sites, just to see what they looked like. I was horrified at what I saw. I would say maybe 4 out of the 40 were actually decent looking sites. The other 90% of the sites were crappy looking.

If you are going to have a website, make it look good. You don't have to be a web designer to do it. Remember, your website is a first impression for 1000's of visitors and if I came across one of these crappy-looking websites, I would not consider purchasing a book from them thinking that their books might be equally as crappy.

Create a game plan for the blog by creating your foundation materials first, then getting blog materials ready for release once or twice a week.

If you are looking for more ideas for content, one of the best ways is to create blogs around the chapters of your book. This is especially effective for non-fiction books. Don't just copy and paste the content of the book into a blog post. Summarize the highlights of the chapters and give selling points to visitors as to why they should purchase your book.

2. Self-host Your Blog/Website
I highly recommend getting your own domain name and your own hosting account. It will cost you less than $100 a year. I say self-host vs. free-hosting because though you can get free hosting from various sources, in my opinion it doesn't have the same feel as a self-hosted blog. I recommend using www.HostingDomainsWeb.com for both the hosting and domain name (I am affiliated with this website as it is a part of my web design business but do not feel any obligation to use it, just offering as a viable solution if you are looking for dependable and reasonable products).

3. Publish the Book as a PDF and Sell on Your Own Website
This process only works if you are not enrolled in Kindle Select. If people come to your site and like your blogs and like the concept of your book, why send them to Amazon to then purchase your book. There are WordPress plug-ins available so that you can sell digital copies of your book online. Payments go through PayPal and a buyer doesn't need to have a PayPal account so that they can pay you. A potential customer can use their credit card to make the payment.

4. Start Affiliate Marketing with Products in Your Book and Website
Affiliate marketing is a way for bloggers or really anyone with a website to make money by promoting other people's' products and/or services. It's quick and easy to do and the best part is that you don't have to worry about inventory or shipping or returns. The goal is to align your book/blog to the right products. This is not an overnight success plan. It takes time to develop followers who will trust you in the products that you promote.

Many bloggers start with the Amazon Associates program because there are millions of products available to promote. Some of them must be related to your book. Other affiliate programs include Commission Junction, LinkShare, and ShareASale. Each one requires a separate application to be filled out.

Important: Your book should be about the niche topic you are writing about, not a "catalog" of products you are selling. Make the book be about the book and the website/blog can offer more information as well as related products.

5. Build an Email List
If you tie your book and website together, over time, you will gain followers and followers have email addresses. Building an email list is crucial towards developing a passive income stream. You can use it for promoting your new books and for promoting any products or services from an affiliate program. There are a bunch of YouTube videos offering help in how to use an email list.

6. Cross Promote Your Books
At the end of your book, you can promote other books that you

have written. What you can do is let's say you finished your second book and would like your first book to promote your second book, you can modify the last page of your first book to include a blurb about the new book and then upload to KDP again. You can send support an email notifying them of the change and if they feel it warrants it, they will email the previous purchasers of your book to let them know of the change.

7. Create an Author's Page on Amazon

Amazon allows you to create your own Author Page. You can write a biography of yourself, add your blog feed, add future events and pictures and videos. All your books will be listed in the same spot so people will be able to have a central place to get your books. Here is my author page for your reference: www.amazon.com/author/jamesgirardi.

9

SUMMARY/CONCLUSION

Arriving at one goal is the starting point to another
~ John Dewey

We covered a lot of ground in this eBook and hopefully you now have the learning tools to successfully research, create, publish and market eBooks via Kindle Direct Publishing.

We learned how to research a profitable niche that will sell by starting with Amazon and researching books that sell in Kindle Books. We learned how to find good categories and research the already successful books in those categories to see if they can become a series and if they have back-end income potential. From there we learned how to outsource the writing of the book as well went over the steps in writing a book. We covered the process for creating a title for your book that will be appealing as well as search engine friendly. Then we worked on how to create an amazing book cover for your book followed by some tools and tips to book writing.

Once the book is complete, we went over the strategies to uploading the book file to Kindle Direct Publishing and how to do the book promotion. Realizing that though the book may be done, our work on the book is not, we discussed how to do a book launch and the various social media platforms to use at our disposal. Finally, we learned how to scale up the business via various income channels like blogs, email lists and affiliate marketing.

I hope you don't stop at one book. I hope you continue the journey and share in the same success. I love to hear about success stories and when you do have your success story, I hope you share it with me. Thank you for your purchase of this book. Reviews are always welcome and appreciated.

Resource to Planning Out Your Website

Since we discussed using websites and blogs for marketing purposes, I would like to share with you another one of my books that discusses the planning process for a website.

The book is entitled, *How to Plan Out Your Web Design: The Plan Before The Plan* and available on Amazon and through my website.

ABOUT THE AUTHOR

James Girardi born and raised on Long Island. After high school, James served in the U.S. Navy and worked on the flight deck of the aircraft carrier, U.S.S. Coral Sea. After his service, he earned an Associates Degree in Liberal Arts then attended Adelphi University and earned a Bachelor's Degree in Business Administration. His work career consisted of various jobs then opened his first business in 1999. Ever since, he has been an entrepreneur, a writer, a sailor, a pilot, a husband and father. James still lives on Long Island and enjoys golf, volleyball, billiards, sailing, writing and web design. More information about James can be found on his website at: www.JamesGirardi.com